W...

Feel Hurt

Dwight L.
Carlson, M.D.

HARVEST HOUSE PUBLISHERS
Eugene, Oregon 97402

WHEN YOU FEEL HURT

Taken from **OVERCOMING HURTS AND ANGER**
Copyright © 1981 by Harvest House Publishers
Eugene, Oregon 97402

ISBN 0-89081-685-9

Preface

As a practicing internist for ten years and then a practicing psychiatrist for 12, I have had the opportunity to care for thousands of patients with every conceivable physical and emotional symptom. They have been people from every walk of life, from every social stratum, and from every religious background. One of the most common causes of their symptoms has been the inability to sense their feelings of anger and deal with these feelings constructively.

There are several viewpoints on how to deal with anger. At one extreme is the currently popular emphasis of giving full vent to one's anger. Psychologists have become increasingly aware of the harmful, long-term effects of repressing anger, so many of them now advocate expressing anger rather than bottling it up, even if expressing it hurts others.

At the other extreme is the view that anger is wrong, and that, therefore, one should be totally passive, a sort of human doormat.

In my opinion, neither of these approaches deals adequately and constructively with anger.

This book presents what I believe to be a balanced approach to the subject and offers guidelines that can help you deal with hurt and anger in ways that are least likely to adversely affect you or those around you. The knowledge and insights shared in this book come not only out of a sound psychological framework, but I believe they are consistent with the Bible, which is a vitally important guideline for myself and for many readers.

—*Dwight L. Carlson*

Dwight L. Carlson, M.D., specializes in both psychiatry and internal medicine. In addition to an active private practice in psychiatry, he is assistant clinical professor in the Department of Psychiatry and Biobehavioral Sciences at UCLA.

1
Mishandling Anger

Camouflaging Anger

Mr. Jones, a 58-year-old executive, sat in my office and told me that he wanted out of his marriage of 32 years. He felt he could cope better with divorce than with this marriage. He described himself as a person who wanted "peace at any price" after yielding for years to the pressures and demands of his wife. He was, as he put it, "always capitulating."

Mr. Jones said that he "faked the harmony" but always resented the deception. He concluded that it would take years to work out the problems in his marriage, and that he didn't have that much time left. For the first 20 years of his married life he hadn't been aware of what was going on. He became conscious of the unhealthy relationship 12 years ago, but hadn't altered his behavior. For the last six months he had been having physical symptoms, but they disappeared three weeks ago, when he told his wife he was leaving.

Mr. Jones illustrates one form that camouflaged anger can take—the don't-make-waves, *peace-at-any-price* individual. This individual will take the blame for anything, even things for which he is in no way responsible. He is self-effacing and never appears to be angry. But the peace is a sham. Often he has psychosomatic complaints which serve as a means of dissipating the anger. Frequently this kind of person is married to someone who expresses his or her feelings more overtly, thus tyrannizing the peace-at-any-price individual. This person may think he is carrying out the Beatitudes because he is always turning the other cheek, but in reality it is a poor counterfeit. Sooner or later the results of this kind of pussyfooting will catch up with him.

Another way a person can camouflage his anger is by becoming a *stamp saver*. This person carefully saves up each little grievance, annoyance, or irritation. He tells himself that each grievance is not enough to deal with in itself. In fact, if asked, he would probably deny that there was anything bothering him at all. He may tell himself that the problem is so small that he shouldn't make an issue of it and that he should be able to forget it.

But in fact he doesn't forget. He pastes a stamp somewhere in his head. When the book gets full, he cashes it in almost gleefully. The last stamp may have been a very minor incident, but out comes pent-up rage that baffles the recipient and sometimes the stamp saver himself. This inappropriate outrage may then be justified by a detailed cataloging of all past offenses.

The third form of camouflage is *the critic*. This individual is critical and sometimes sarcastic about everything. Often his criticisms are supported by seemingly well-founded intellectual or rational reasoning, but through it all something seems wrong, and one can sense an undertone of anger, hostility, and negativism.

Another form that camouflaged anger can take is that of the *passive-aggressive* person. This kind of person is characterized by aggressive behavior exhibited in passive ways such as pouting, stubbornness, and procrastination. He often takes the opposite point of view or opposes other people's actions. If you say you like jogging, he will tell you how dangerous jogging can be. The next day if you say you don't like jogging, he'll tell you it's a great sport and everybody should take it up. If you say something is white, he'll call it black; if you say it's black, he'll say it's white. Such people are often late and keep others waiting for them. The passive-aggressive person tends to be a drag on others. Prolonged contact with this kind of person can be extremely frustrating.

Repressing Anger

Many people who think that anger is wrong don't stop with just camouflaging it. They actually convince themselves that there is no anger in their lives. This denial of anger often occurs at an unconscious level, so that the people are unaware that they're doing this. They then try to convince others that they aren't angry. We're all familiar with the person who snaps, "No, I'm not angry!" when quite obviously he is. However, in some cases, the person who protests that he isn't angry is quite calm and collected and actually feels no anger. He may have repressed his anger to such a degree that he is completely numb to his feelings, while in reality a great deal of anger is buried underneath.

Anger, in my opinion, is like energy. It cannot be destroyed, but it can be stored or its form can be changed. When we bury the anger within us and repeatedly deny its existence, it accumulates in what I have chosen to call an *unresolved anger fund*. The more we push down anger, the more it accumulates. This accumulated anger will then express itself through any of the camouflages previously described, or it may convert its energy to less recognizable forms. It can lead to tremendous guilt, obesity, or insomnia. It can manifest itself in psychosomatic illnesses like backache, dermatological conditions, headaches, gastrointestinal symptoms, and ulcers. Other possible manifestations are sexual problems and fatigue.

In addition to the physical symptoms created by bottled-up anger, there are the more obvious emotional symptoms like depressions, neuroses, psychoses, and potential for murder and suicide. This is not to imply that unresolved hurts and anger are the sole cause of all these symptoms, but they are certainly a major cause.

Recently I heard a psychiatrist speak who had examined hundreds of prisoners charged or convicted of murder. He said that 70 to 80 percent of the prisoners hadn't wanted to hurt anyone, and that they didn't seem to get angry or to have any problem with anger. They were often law-abiding citizens who didn't even have a traffic ticket to their record. What happened? In my opinion, these people didn't know how to recognize and deal constructively with small amounts of anger, and so they allowed it to build in their unresolved anger fund. One slight provocation was then enough to fill the fund to the top and make them explode, usually on someone they knew.

The Overtly Angry Person

As noted in the two preceding sections, anger may be camouflaged or it may be denied so that the person is totally unaware of his own feelings.

The polar opposite of the person who denies anger is the person who is overtly angry. This person can be either chronically hostile or may have only occasional violent bursts of temper. Most talks, books, or sermons on anger are directed toward the person with this kind of anger. The church appropriately tells the chronically hostile person that his behavior needs changing. However, the sermon usually ends at that point, leaving the person to figure out on his own what is going on in his life and how to achieve that change in behavior. In addition, most of the people sitting in the pews handle their anger by repressing it, and thus the sermon doesn't help either group of individuals—those who are overtly angry or those who repress their anger.

Joe comes to mind in this context. Joe's concern was that people often tell him how hostile he is. He said that even strangers comment on his temper, one example being a waitress who had known him for only three minutes. He told me that he is sometimes aware that he is "slightly angry," but not to the extent or degree that people tell him. Often he seems angry when he sees me for therapy, but if I ask him if he is, he denies it.

Since we have just discussed in such great detail the evils of camouflaging and denying anger, you might think that someone who expresses his anger as much as Joe does would be blissfully happy. But that isn't the case at all—Joe is chronically unhappy. He is frequently suicidal, and he has ostracized himself from almost all his friends and relatives.

During a recent appointment, Joe related how furious he was at his boss for criticizing his work one day. When I asked him how he had handled the situation, he said that he had felt the criticism was totally unjustified, but that he hadn't expressed his feelings to his boss. He kept them in, but remained very upset all day. However, when he went home that night, he blew up at his wife over a very inconsequential matter. The following day he had lunch with his boss and some employees. Some of the boss's comments sounded prejudiced to Joe, so he angrily criticized him in front of the other workers, calling him a bigot. This made Joe feel a little better because he had released his anger, but several days later in my office he was still licking his emotional wounds.

Let's take a look at the scorecard. I don't know if the boss's criticism was justified or not. Let's assume that the boss was wrong. The initial hurt and anger from the original insult had not been dealt with constructively, either by talking it over with the boss or by reconciling it within himself. Then he had created problems at home by taking out his frustrations on his family. In addition, criticizing his boss at lunch only further complicated the situation. None of his actions led to any resolution of the initial problem. In fact, they only intensified his problems, and a few weeks later Joe impetuously quit his job because he couldn't handle the pressures there any longer. This placed further strain on his horrible financial situation and led him very close to committing suicide. Thus, expressing his anger was not the answer. His need was to handle his anger in a constructive way.

2

Biblical Principles

The Contradiction

I'm sure many of you are saying, "Wait a minute—are you saying anger is *right*? How do you explain away the verses in the Bible that say anger is a sin?"

Some verses do say that anger is wrong. Ephesians 4:31 says, "Let all . . . anger . . . be put away." Psalm 37:8 says, "Cease from anger," and the Sermon on the Mount teaches, "If you are only *angry*, even in your own home, you are in danger of judgment" (Matthew 5:22 TLB).

On the other hand, some parts of the Bible seem to condone anger. Perhaps the most striking verses to this effect are Psalm 4:4 and Ephesians 4:26. Psalm 4:4 reads, "Be angry, but sin not" (RSV). The same thought is repeated in Ephesians 4:26: "Be angry, and yet do not sin." One commentator writes, "The words 'be ye angry' are a present imperative in the Greek text, commanding a continuous action" (*Wuest's Word Studies from the Greek New Testament for the*

English Reader, page 114). Thus it can almost be construed as a command to be angry under certain conditions.

A careful study of the Bible reveals that most of the important characters in it got angry, contrary to the stereotypes we have of them today. Moses was a patriarch who without question was blessed of God. However, he sometimes became extremely angry. For example, when Moses returned from receiving the Ten Commandments and the Law from God on Mount Sinai, he discovered that in his absence the Israelites had started worshiping idols. He became so enraged that he smashed the stone tablets on which the Law was written (Exodus 32:19).

David was described as a man after God's own heart (Acts 13:22), yet he became angry at God when a man was killed trying to protect the ark of God (2 Samuel 6:6-8).

We could cite dozens of verse in which men of God got angry. However, we still might not be able to conclude anything, because it could be argued that they were sinning in each case. For example, one could argue that while Moses should indeed have reprimanded the Israelites, he should not have let himself get so carried away that he smashed the sacred Law of God.

Nevertheless, there are two Personages in the Bible whom we cannot accuse of sinning when they got angry.

Do you know who in the Bible got angry the most often? Not the Pharisees, nor the Philistines, nor any other assorted heathen. It was God Himself—God, who is without sin. The Hebrew word for anger appears approximately 455 times in the Old Testament, and 375 of these times refer to the anger of God.

Jesus also became quite angry at times, contrary to the image we have of Him as a bland, quiet soul. He got upset when He saw the hard hearts of the people as He was about to heal the man with a paralyzed hand (Mark 3:1-5). In Mark 11:15-17 we find Him driving out the parasitic money changers in the temple with a whip. In Matthew 23 He lashes out at the smug, hypocritical Pharisees, calling them "whitewashed tombs . . . full of dead men's bones!"

Thus some verses indicate that we shouldn't be angry, while others seem to tell us that if we are to follow Christ's and God's examples, there are times when we should be angry. How can we reconcile one verse in which God Himself is angry with another verse in which God commands us not to be angry?

Biblical Analysis

Studying the meanings of the various words for anger in the original languages in which the Bible was written might shed considerable light upon this matter. For example, there could be one word for anger which denotes God's justified anger, meaning a sort of detached, righteous indignation, while a different word could be used for Saul's unjustified anger when he tried to kill David, meaning a malicious, vindictive rage (1 Samuel 19:10).

The Hebrew word most frequently translated "anger" comes from the word *aph*. This word appears several hundred times in the Hebrew Old Testament. It is usually used to describe God's obviously appropriate anger, such as appears in Numbers 11:1: "Now the people became like those who complain of adversity in the hearing of the Lord; and when the Lord heard it, His anger was kindled, and the fire of the Lord burned among them and consumed some of . . . the camp." This same word *aph* describes Moses' strong but questionable emotions when he smashed the stone tablets against the mountain.

Not only is this word used to describe God's appropriate anger and Moses' questionable anger, but it is also the word used to denote clearly inappropriate anger, as in the case of Balaam (Numbers 22:27). Thus exactly the same word is used to describe appropriate, questionable, and inappropriate anger.

When we turn to the New Testament, one of the more common words translated "anger" is *orge*. This Greek word originally referred to any natural impulse, desire, or disposition. Later it came to signify anger. It was thought of as an internal motion, like the juices in plants or fruit, and meant the natural disposition, temper, character, or impulse of a thing. Just as in the Old Testament, this word is sometimes used to describe appropriate anger, such as God's or Christ's (Hebrews 3:11; Romans 9:22; Mark 3:5). Yet it is the same word that is translated "anger" in Ephesians 4:31: "Let all bitterness and wrath and anger and clamor and slander be put away from you, along with all malice." Thus this word is also used to describe both appropriate and inappropriate anger.

The Logical Conclusion

I believe that the logical conclusion we can draw is that each of the words translated "anger" is used in neutral, negative, or positive ways, and that we must look at the context of each verse to see whether the anger is justified or not.

Likewise, in our own lives we must look at the context of each situation to judge whether our anger is justified or not. Anger is *in and of itself* neutral; it is neither right nor wrong, appropriate nor inappropriate, holy nor sinful. Nor has it anything to do with how intense the anger is. In some cases we may actually be sinning by only being mildly irritated when it may be God's will for us to be very angry.

It is what the anger is based on and how the anger is expressed that determines whether it is right or wrong. This parallels perfectly the usual psychological view of anger, which is that anger is an emotion that is in itself neutral but which may have an inappropriate or an appropriate basis, and that anger may be used destructively or constructively.

Biblical Principles About Anger

The Scriptures offer many guidelines for handling anger properly. First of all, it should be understood that feelings of anger, as well as feelings of all kinds, are God-given gifts. According to Genesis 1:26,27, God in His wisdom created us in His own image, and it is my belief that one of the things He created us with was the ability to get angry. Feelings can be used to serve us and to serve God as well. To deny them is to deny a part of the person God created us to be.

I believe that the Scriptures teach that if we deny our anger we are in fact sinning. Whether the basis for the anger is right or wrong is immaterial at this point. If anger exists and you deny its presence to yourself or others, you are living a lie. That is sin. Even if you know that in a particular situation it is wrong for you to be angry, to lie about it is to add one sin upon another. In addition, denying our anger vastly complicates working out the problem with our fellow human beings. In Ephesians 4:25 we read, "Therefore, laying aside falsehood, speak truth, each one of you, with his neighbor, for we are members of one another."

A crucial principle is that a person should listen to his feelings but never be controlled by them. James 1:19 says, "Let everyone be quick to hear, slow to speak and slow to anger."

Just as we should not be in a hurry to deal with anger, we must also not go to the opposite extreme and delay longer than is necessary. This is an extremely important point. If you are in a situation with another person in which you react with feelings of hurt or anger, and you know that you need to talk to that individual about it, it is far preferable to take the appropriate action in a matter of seconds or minutes (or at the most a few hours after the incident) than to wait days, weeks, months, or even years before constructively handling the situation.

Ephesians 4:26 is very applicable to this problem—"Be angry, and yet do not sin; do not let the sun go down on your anger." Not letting the sun go down on your anger seems to have three possible interpretations. First of all, the usual interpretation is that it is referring to *time*—that is, that we should resolve or deal with the anger the same day or at least in very close proximity to the event which caused the anger.

According to Vine's *Expository Dictionary of New Testament Words* (Volume III, p. 93), the word *helios*, which is translated "the sun," can also mean "the natural benefits of light and heat . . . and judgment." Thus it seems that an alternate rendering might be, "Don't wait so long in dealing with the anger that the intensity of the *feeling* decreases and sets within you before you take appropriate action." I believe it can be useful to deal with the issue while you still feel angry, if certain stipulations are met which will be discussed in detail later.

Several verses in the Bible refer to the day as the time of *opportunity* (John 9:4). Thus a third possible interpretation is that we should deal with our feelings while there is still an opportunity.

In summary, a possible interpretation of Ephesians 4:26 might read like this: "It's appropriate and necessary to be angry, but be very careful that you don't sin in the process. Dissipate the anger constructively before the heat of the emotion is lost, too much time passes, and the best opportunity is gone."

Another principle taught in the Scriptures is that when you are angry you are much more vulnerable to sin. Proverbs 29:22 warns, "An angry man stirs up strife, and a hot-tempered man abounds in transgression." Proverbs 14:29 adds, "A wise man controls his temper. He knows that anger causes mistakes" (TLB).

Another translation of Ephesians 4:26 focuses on the danger of nursing our anger and letting it turn into bitterness and resentment: "If you are angry, do not let anger lead you into sin; do not let sunset find you still nursing it; leave no loophole for the devil" (NEB). The Scriptures teach that the persistent anger which makes us bitter and resentful is probably always sin. Hebrews 12:15 says, "See to it . . . that no root of bitterness springing up causes trouble, and by it many be defiled."

We mechanically repeat the part of the Lord's Prayer that says "Forgive us our debts, as we forgive our debtors," but very few of us stop to consider the consequences of what we are saying. The Amplified Bible's interpretation of the verse immediately following the Lord's Prayer says that if we do not give up our resentment, God will not forgive our sins (Matthew 6:15). Thus, clinging stubbornly to resentment is very destructive to the person himself, because it blocks God's forgiveness.

The Scriptures also teach that vindictive, malicious anger is wrong. Almost every time the phrase "cease from anger" is found in the Bible, it is in the context of wrath or vindictiveness. For example, Psalm 37:8 says, "Cease from anger, and forsake wrath." Romans 12:18,19 says, "If possible, so far as it depends on you, be at peace with all men. Never take your own revenge, beloved, but leave room for the wrath of God, for it is written, 'Vengeance is Mine, I will repay, says the Lord.' "

The final principle—and perhaps the most startling one—is that in some cases anger may be righteous and its absence may displease God. In other words, we may be sinning by not getting angry. First Samuel 11:6 reads, "Then the Spirit of God came upon Saul mightily when he heard these words, and he became very angry." The passage goes on to indicate that Saul's anger and the resulting action he took were appropriate and righteous. In Nehemiah 5:6-9, a prophet, speaking as God's messenger, became angry at the people as he reprimanded them for their sin. God even commanded Moses to be angry, in Numbers 25:16,17: "The Lord spoke to Moses, saying, 'Be hostile to the Midianites and strike them.' "

Have you ever considered the possibility that Christ might have been sinning if he hadn't gotten angry at the moneychangers in the temple? There are other examples in the Scriptures of people who probably were sinning because they didn't get angry enough to do anything. For example, while Moses was receiving the Ten Commandments from God on Mount Sinai, Aaron was completely passive when the Israelites demanded that he make an idol for them to worship. Exodus 32:25 says, "The people were out of control, for Aaron had let them get out of control." Aaron would have been better off if he had had some of Moses' tablet-smashing anger!

The church leaders at Corinth probably would not have received such a strong rebuke from Paul if they had stirred up enough anger to take appropriate action against the incestuous church member (see 1 Corinthians 5). Considering these examples, another rendering of "Be angry but do not sin" might be "Be appropriately angry and thereby do not sin." In my opinion, many people don't get angry when they should and therefore do not mobilize the energy necessary to deal with some crucially important issues of life.

3

Handling Your Anger

Principles about anger are fine, but what are you supposed to do when you actually get angry? What are you supposed to do when someone snaps at you or insults you, and suddenly you feel hurt, your jaw tenses, and angry retorts flash through your head?

I have outlined a step-by-step procedure to draw upon in problem situations like this.

Recognize Your Feelings of Displeasure

The first step is to get in touch with your feelings of hurt, displeasure, or anger. At this point in the proceedings, *do not judge* the cause of the feeling as to whether it is reasonable or not, or even as to whether it is right or wrong. Here you are identifying the presence of hurt or feelings of anger only. This step can be compared to looking at the temperature gauge on the dashboard of your car; you aren't determining the cause of the overheated engine, but are only aware of the fact that it is overheated.

Suppress Taking Any Action

The second step is to suppress taking any action until you have *thought through* the situation and have *control* of what you say and do. Suppressing action is not the same as repressing anger. When a person represses anger, he buries it and often isn't aware of his feelings at all. However, suppressing anger means that you defer taking action without losing touch with the problem. It is akin to the proverbial "counting to ten." Sometimes this step may take only seconds or minutes, but in some cases it may take hours or possibly days.

The Bible encourages us not to be hasty in dealing with our anger. Proverbs 29:11 says, "A fool gives full vent to his anger, but a wise man quietly holds it back" (RSV).

I have already stated that you should not take any action at this stage in the proceedings. However, if you find yourself in a situation in which you suddenly have some angry feelings that aren't altogether clear to you yet, and someone asks you if you're upset, the temptation will be to say, "No, it didn't bother me." If in reality you were bothered, saying that you weren't would be dishonest and make it more difficult to deal with the incident with that person later on, should the need arise.

It would be better to say something like, "Yes, what you said did upset me, but I'll have to think

it through before I say anything more about it."
Or you might tag the situation by saying, "Something about that bothers me, but it's not clear to
me yet. Maybe when I've had a chance to think it
over we can talk about it." Tagging the situation
marks it as a problem to you and the other person, but you are consciously deferring any defin-
itive action. It also alerts the other person to
think about what was said and done and decreases
the chance that he will forget about it, which
might further anger you and make dealing with
it more difficult.

If you don't tag the situation verbally, it is
crucial that you at least tag it in your mind. As a
result, if there are some other urgent tasks at
hand when you become aware that something is
bothering you, you will have pinned the problem down in your mind and committed yourself
to coming back to deal with it later. If you don't
tag the situation, it is very possible that you will
forget the specific issue that caused you to feel
upset. Then if you feel vaguely upset later, you
won't know why and you may be unable to resolve the problem. Doing this repeatedly can
cause all kinds of havoc and can add to your
unresolved anger fund.

It pays to remember that timing is very important in dealing with emotional issues. I've already
mentioned that it is essential to wait before taking action until you have thought through the
situation and have adequate control of both your
words and actions. I want to emphasize that I am
not saying that you must have control of all of
your feelings, whether primary or secondary

feelings. In fact, at times it is useful to take action when there are still some feelings present, because they can help you take the necessary action.

However, I'm not at all suggesting the expression of excessive anger by extreme means. A patient once told me about an incident that is applicable to this issue. She had had many psychiatric hospitalizations, and one of the contributing factors to her problem was an uncooperative, fully grown son who had been freeloading off her for years. Once, when she was feeling worse and was going to be admitted to a psychiatric hospital, her son seemed very pleased at the prospect of getting rid of her. This made her so furious that she marched back into the house with her suitcases and told her son to get out of the house and support himself.

This may not have been the most mature way to handle the problem, but for her it was progress, and it is a graphic example of how emotional energy can be used in positive ways. This same thing happened when the Spirit of God came upon Saul, causing him to become very angry and to move into action (1 Samuel 11:6,7).

In this step of suppressing action (because we don't want to take premature action), we don't want to delay unnecessarily either. Every minute that unresolved conflict is carried inside, it extracts a tremendous toll on a person's life. You should suppress taking action until the above criteria are met, but thereafter action should be taken as soon as possible. At first, learning to identify your feelings and thinking through the situation may take days, weeks, or even months.

But later you will be able to go through this step more quickly, usually at the time of the initial hurt.

Pray

It would seem appropriate to mention how helpful a prayerful attitude of dependency on God can be, particularly in stressful situations. Simply stating, "Lord, help me see the issues more clearly" or "Lord, help me sort out my thoughts and feelings so I can do the right thing" cannot be overemphasized.

I don't believe that a person necessarily has to pray specifically in each and every little situation that arises, but I do believe this should be the general desire of the heart. On the other hand, there may be many occasions in which a person will want to draw away from the crowd to pray specifically about a situation.

Identify the Cause of Your Anger

What is it that is making you feel upset or angry? What is causing your anger? What is the primary feeling leading to the angry feelings? What is being threatened? Answering these questions is the next step. Many times the cause of the anger is very obvious, so this step is no problem at all.

However, people who have difficulty understanding and dealing with their feelings may have considerable difficulty with this step. If you get angry at your ten-year-old son for leaving his bike in the driveway, you need to consider whether you are really angry with your child or whether the true cause of your anger is the boss who chewed you out at work or the man who cut you off on the freeway or some combination thereof. Anger can so easily be displaced to someone with whom it is safer to express that bottled-up feeling. I'm sure you are all familiar with the following chain reaction: The boss yells at his employee, who gets angry at his wife, who then takes it out on her son, who in turn kicks the dog.

This procedure of taking out one's anger on a weaker creature is not unique to human beings; it has even been documented in laboratory animals. Probably the first recorded incident of the displacement of anger onto a defenseless animal is found in Numbers 22, where Balaam became angry at his donkey instead of realizing that he was upset because God wouldn't cooperate with his plan.

I know of people who are stymied at this step because they have difficulty in figuring out what made them so angry. Each of them in his or her own way has to pause to determine the sequence of events leading up to the anger. One person will need to take a piece of paper and write until the issues are clarified. Another may have to talk over the problem with a close friend. Still another may need professional help to identify the source of his angry feelings. But whatever it takes to do the job, you cannot proceed any further until the cause of the displeasure is identified.

Is Your Anger Legitimate?

Nehemiah said, "I was very angry when I heard their cry and these words. I thought it over, then rebuked the nobles and officials" (Nehemiah 5:6,7 AMP). Here Nehemiah was able to get in touch with his feelings, to think through the situation, and then to take the appropriate action of rebuking the leaders. Elsewhere in the Scriptures we find, "Then God said to Jonah, 'Do you have good reason to be angry?' " (Jonah 4:9). In this case God was questioning Jonah as to whether he had an adequate basis for his angry feelings. It turned out that Jonah didn't have just cause for his anger.

This reminds me of the day my 13-year-old son came whizzing past me in the breakfast room and greeted me with the words, "Hi, Chubby." He wasn't even out of the room by the time I could sense that I was hurt and starting to get angry. I was just about ready to say something when I realized that there was some truth in what he had just said, so I delayed taking action.

As I thought about it, I became aware that the legitimacy of the statement was what made it hurt; what made me so mad was the fact that he was right. I had been telling myself for the past six months that I should be working on my weight. I concluded that he was right and that I had no legitimate basis for getting upset with him, and soon my feelings of hurt and anger subsided. If he had a habit of saying things like that it would have been a different matter, but this had been the only time he had ever made such a comment, and so I let it pass.

It is interesting to note that within a week a colleague of mine at work said to me, "You ought to lose some weight, Dwight." This time I was able to agree with him, saying "You know, you're right." And this feeling of displeasure with my weight spurred me on to lose 20 pounds.

Determine a Course of Action

At any of the above steps, you may have been able to resolve the problem. If that is the case, so much the better, and the steps that follow will not be necessary for you. However, if the problem is not resolved, then you will need to take further action to handle your feelings constructively, lest they turn into a destructive force against you or others.

Most people deal with conflict by one of the following methods: 1) They angrily attack—"I'll get even with him"; 2) they run or withdraw—"I'll take my marbles and go home"; 3) they verbally give in to the other person—"Okay, you win"; but in reality they are unhappy with the situation. People who use the latter two methods typically harbor resentment.

In spite of the fact that all of the above methods are grossly inadequate in dealing with conflicts, many people still rely heavily upon them. What people need to know is that there is a large array of skills available to them for the handling of situations in which there is conflict. They need to become proficient in selecting the best means of handling a given situation. The following are specific courses of action that one can take when conflict arises.

Confront when necessary

Anyone who really cares about people and their feelings finds confrontation difficult, but a mature person will confront someone when it is necessary. In 2 Corinthians 2:4, Paul shares with his readers how he felt about having to confront them: "Oh, how I hated to write that letter! It almost broke my heart, and I tell you honestly that I cried over it. I didn't want to hurt you, but I had to show you how very much I loved you and cared about what was happening to you" (TLB).

There are many examples of confrontation in the Scriptures. Probably the first example that comes to mind is when Jesus sharply attacked the Pharisees in Mark 7. It is interesting to note that even Jesus' disciples couldn't understand His remarks to the religious leaders, and on one occasion they came to Him and said, "You offended the Pharisees by that remark" (Matthew 15:12 TLB). But Jesus did not retract His statements because He had fully intended to confront them.

Jesus also rebuked Peter sharply in Matthew 16:23. We find that Paul "had great dissension and debate" with some men from Judea regarding religious customs (Acts 15:2). Paul also opposed Peter "to his face" because Peter was wrong on a certain issue (Galatians 2:11).

Confrontation isn't necessarily a hostile, painful experience; it can also be done in a tender and forgiving manner. One example of this kind of confrontation is the way Jesus treated the adulterous woman whom the Pharisees wanted to stone to death. Jesus told the Pharisees, "Let him who is without sin among you cast the first stone." One by one the Pharisees slipped away. Jesus then turned to the woman and said, "Where are your accusers? . . . Go, and sin no more" (John 8:10,11 TLB).

Whenever possible, it is best that confrontation be done in private. If a problem has developed between you and another individual, endeavor to resolve it between the two of you alone, without involving others. Matthew 18:15 says, "If a brother sins against you, go to him privately and confront him with his fault" (TLB).

There are several exceptions to this. First, if others have observed the conflict or were in some way involved, it may need to be resolved with these individuals present. Another time that you may want to involve others is if a person refuses to deal with you alone, yet you feel that an important principle or issue is at stake that requires resolution. The passage in Matthew 18:15 continues, "If he listens and confesses it, you have won back a brother. But if not, then take one or two others with you and go back to him again, proving everything you say by these witnesses. If he still refuses to listen, then take your case to the church" (verses 16, 17 TLB). Though it is preferable not to involve others, there are some occasions when it is necessary, as when the problem can't be resolved adequately without them.

Confrontation can thus vary widely from a very gentle, private resolution of an issue to a strong, possibly unpleasant situation involving others. There are three general ways to confront people: 1) to inform; 2) to share your primary feelings; and 3) to rebuke in love.

Inform the other person

We often overlook or fail to *inform* another person clearly and honestly about our feelings on an issue that affects us. For example, the simple statement "You're stepping on my foot" is usually the best way to inform a person in a crowded elevator that he is hurting you and that you would like him to stop. Often the person isn't even aware that he is stepping on your foot unless you quietly inform him of the fact. To angrily snap, "You're stepping on my foot, you clod!" only complicates the situation. Another example of informing is saying to the person who cuts in front of you, "The line forms over there." Even if the person has deliberately taken advantage of you, usually a simple statement resolves the situation effectively.

When we feel something strongly, it is up to us to express it. *We are asking for all kinds of trouble if we assume that the other person knows how strongly we feel, unless we actually put it into words and express our feelings directly to the person involved.*

My wife and I have been guilty in the past of inadequately informing each other of our feelings, and we continue to find it necessary to work on this area of our marriage. I recall an incident that occurred nine years ago that made us acutely aware of the need to share our feelings. I was extremely busy with a full practice and was on many hospital and church-related committees. Often I would leave home early in the morning, before the family had breakfast, and would arrive home late at night, after everyone was in bed. No doubt I was in error for being so busy, and for that reason I was not tuned in to Betty's needs. Betty, on the other hand, not wanting to bother me with her needs because I was so busy, only hinted quietly of her need to talk with me, hints which I honestly didn't hear.

One day a friend confronted Betty with her responsibility to inform me of her turmoil, even if it meant making an appointment with me in my office. Finally Betty wrote me a note and left it on my desk to open the channels of communication, but unfortunately she went through some very painful weeks before she informed me, and by that time it had created some deep hurts for both of us.

Convey primary feelings

The second way to confront is to *convey your primary feelings*. Anger itself is a secondary feeling or reaction to some insult, threat, putdown, or frustration of our wishes. The initial or primary feeling is hurt, belittlement, or frustration, to name a few typical ones. For example, if someone stomps on your foot, you first feel pain, which is followed by anger and the urge to push the person off your foot. Each step in this God-given process is vital. The primary feeling of pain is the protective warning signal. The secondary feeling, anger, enables you to take protective actions against the offender. One of the most constructive ways of dealing with anger is to get in touch with the primary feeling and then to share this with the person you need to confront.

This is best exemplified by sending an *I Feel* message. *I Feel* messages are a beautiful way of sharing how you feel, and they often help everyone involved to get in touch with their primary feelings. Below are some examples of *I Feel* messages, as contrasted to *Blaming You* messages.

I Feel Messages	*Blaming You* Messages
1. I'm feeling ignored	You're making me mad because you're paying so much attention to Mary.
2. I feel disappointed that I can't go too.	You're making me angry by deliberately leaving me behind.
3. I get the feeling that I'm being blamed for that.	You always blame me for everything that goes wrong.
4. I feel put down.	You're always putting me down.

I Feel **Messages**	*Blaming You* **Messages**
5. I feel like I'm being interrogated.	Why are you finding fault with me again?

In contrast to the *I Feel* messages, *Blaming You* messages usually begin with the word *you* and often include an accusation. They frequently assume the intent, motivation, and feelings of the other person. Even if the *Blaming You* message is correct, it is usually difficult to defend. Such messages sound judgmental, critical, attacking, and final, giving no room for the other person to respond. They tend to raise the hostilities and defenses of the other person, a process which often happens unconsciously. Only the extremely mature person can receive a *Blaming You* message and turn it into a constructive interaction.

Rebuke in Love

The third and strongest way to confront is to *rebuke in love*. Here you are telling the person directly that what he is saying or doing is inappropriate. Note, however, that the rebuke is given in love, which differentiates it from the angry attack. Because you care about the person you are rebuking, the aim of rebuking in love is reconciliation. You may dislike or even hate what the person is doing, but you do care about the person. Proverbs 27:5,6 says, "Open rebuke is better than hidden love! Wounds from a friend are better than kisses from an enemy!" (TLB). Eli probably sinned because "he did not rebuke" his sons. He only meekly questioned them when they disregarded God's laws of worship (1 Samuel 3:13).

One word of warning regarding confrontation: Some people are afraid of confronting someone because they don't know if they will be able to control their anger. If someone feels violently angry, he may have to put off confrontation and get some help, perhaps even professional help, so that he will eventually be able to confront the person without physically harming him.

Establish limits of behavior

Kristine, a 31-year-old patient of mine, sought my help because of depression. She has two boys, ages eight and ten, with whom she is frequently angry. For example, John, the ten-year-old, frequently leaves his bicycle outside the back door, requiring others to walk around it. Several times Kristine stumbled over it. Kristine is aware of her anger over this and she certainly confronts John, but it is with yelling and screaming, and it doesn't seem to be accomplishing very much.

Last week we talked about setting limits on what is and what is not acceptable behavior, and how to utilize appropriate consequences. Guess what—the next day Kristine was carrying a large box from the house to the garage, and she didn't see John's bike. She stumbled and dropped the box. As the adrenalin started to surge, so did her yelling.

Then she remembered our session of the previous day. Her rage decreased and she firmly called John. She explained what had just happened and how she might have injured herself or damaged items in the box. Then she clearly and firmly told John that she would take the box to the garage and that she expected the bike to be removed by the time she returned. If it wasn't removed, she would remove it, and if she ever had to take that action again the bike would be locked up for a week. This would mean he would have to walk a mile-and-a-half to and from school and wouldn't be able to play with his bike after school—something very important to him.

As Kristine walked to the garage she was amazed at how quickly her angry feelings had subsided. Normally an incident such as this would have ruined the rest of her day, and possibly also the day for the entire family. When she returned to the house the bike was gone, and it has not been left at the back door since then. Kristine was amazed at how well this resolved the problem, compared with her previous habit of yelling. She had established a limit of behavior with predetermined consequences, which negated her anger and produced the desired results.

Limit-setting with predetermined consequences can be used in any situation in which one has the right and/or responsibility over others. This is especially true for parents, teachers, and employers. Keep in mind, however, that when setting limits the rules or limits should be fair and consistently applied, all parties should know the consequences before the infraction is done, and the limit-setter must follow through on the consequences.

Get counsel

Another way to handle negative feelings is to seek counsel. At times all of us find ourselves in need of someone with whom we can talk over a problem. This person need not be a professional; sometimes a friend, spouse, or peer who can help clarify issues and give objectivity to a problem is all that we need. In any case, this person should be fairly mature and a good listener, and shouldn't be prone to give quick answers. He should be a confidant who won't gossip about your problem or use it against you. Some people may need to get counsel from a professional. This is especially true of a person who might lose control of himself if he started getting in touch with his anger or other deep feelings. As mentioned previously, praying is certainly advisable at this point and can be an invaluable means of getting counsel from God, the Great Counselor (See James 1:5).

Compromise when appropriate

Seldom when we get angry are we 100 percent right and the other person 100 percent wrong. Typically, there are multiple factors causing the problem and several different ways to view the situation. Often after we have gone through some of the steps for handling anger, particularly the step of confrontation, we become aware of the other person's feelings, and suddenly we are faced with a different perspective on the issue. The ability to compromise is an integral characteristic of the emotionally and spiritually mature person (See Acts 15:1-29).

While we don't want our feelings to be ignored and trampled underfoot, neither do we want to do the same to the other person.

Pass over the issue

At times we must learn to pass over the issue. This is not repression, which is denying the existence of a significant problem and burying any accompanying feelings. Though it is somewhat similar to withdrawing, the internal feelings and the basis are different. The basis for passing over the issue is realizing that the best possible solution to the problem, both for ourselves and for the other person, is to simply drop the issue. It means that we *hold no grudges*, that we are *willing to forgive and forget*.

Passing over an issue involves a *full awareness* of the injury done to us and a deliberate willingness to *completely* drop the charges against the person(s) who has hurt us. We may decide that we don't have a good case or that it's not worth the expense to us and the other person to press charges.

For example, I have found that I can choose whether to react with or without anger to a scratch or dent somebody makes in my car. Sure, I don't like scratches on my car, but I also realize that a car is only a material possession and often is not worth the emotional trauma. That doesn't mean that I would never take the name of the party at fault and try to get him to pay for the damages. It merely means that there are times when I may choose to pass over the anger-producing problem. I am also finding that as I become more mature I am able to pass over more conflicts.

The other night as I started to back out of the parking lot at work, I noticed that one headlight wasn't working. I got out of the car to see why and discovered that it was smashed. The car parked in front of me had a high bumper that could easily have smashed the headlight when squeezing into the tight spot in front of me. But when I thought about what a hassle it would be to try to find the owner and to confront him, I chose to drop the issue. I drove home and the next day paid $24.95 to replace the light. That was a bargain in comparison to the time and conflict it might otherwise have cost.

We must choose our battles. The world is filled with injustices and irritants. Jesus chose to deal with the Pharisees at certain times, but He also passed over many other issues that He legitimately could have fought. For example, slavery was common in those days, but He chose not to deal with that issue. Also, the country was occupied by Roman soldiers at that time, but He didn't deal with that issue either.

Proverbs 19:11 says, "The discretion of a man deferreth his anger, and it is his glory to pass over a transgression" (KJV). First Peter 2:23 points out that Jesus could accept unjust treatment and let it pass because He knew that God would someday judge the entire situation righteously and would take action against the person who had wronged Him.

Review the Process

The diagram on the next page summarizes the steps for handling anger constructively. On the left side of the page we have the initial hurt or anger. Moving to the right on the diagram, the first step is to recognize those hurt or angry feelings and to evaluate how strong they are. The second step is to suppress taking any action until you have thought through the problem adequately and are sure you have full control of your words and actions.

I have listed Step 3 as praying or having a prayerful attitude, one of "Lord, help me." It almost goes without saying that it is appropriate to stop and pray at any point in the proceedings. Thus this step has been enclosed in brackets to indicate that it is optional and can be used at any step in the sequence.

The fourth step is to identify the reason for your anger, to find out what is really upsetting you, to find the root cause of the problem. The fifth step is to evaluate whether your anger has a legitimate basis; that is, are the person's criticisms or actions valid, or are they unjustified? If you do have a legitimate cause for your anger, then you have to decide on one of the appropriate courses of action outlined in Step 6.

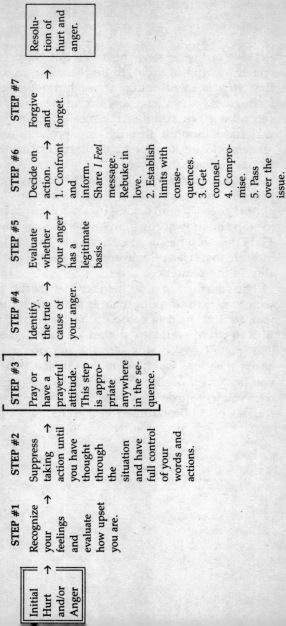

| Initial Hurt and/or Anger | → | **STEP #1** Recognize your feelings and evaluate how upset you are. | → | **STEP #2** Suppress taking action until you have thought through the situation and have full control of your words and actions. | → | **STEP #3** Pray or have a prayerful attitude. This step is appropriate anywhere in the sequence. | → | **STEP #4** Identify the true cause of your anger. | → | **STEP #5** Evaluate whether your anger has a legitimate basis. | → | **STEP #6** Decide on action. 1. Confront and inform. Share *I Feel* message. Rebuke in love. 2. Establish limits with consequences. 3. Get counsel. 4. Compromise. 5. Pass over the issue. | → | **STEP #7** Forgive and forget. | → | Resolution of hurt and anger. |

The various options in Step 6 are confrontation, establishing limits of behavior with consequences, getting counsel, compromising, or passing over the issue. A combination of these courses of action is also possible. For example, you might get some counseling, then confront the individual, and then compromise.

It is important to point out that each of these steps or skills will be necessary to use at one time or another. The particular means you choose will depend on the given situation and your ability to think through and select the best course of action. We must be familiar with and able to use each of these skills or we will run into difficulty. Not being able to draw on a particular skill when it is needed is a gigantic handicap.

When Step 6 is completed, you *must* move on to Step 7, which is forgiving and forgetting. This should lead naturally to the resolution of your hurt or angry feelings and often the resolution of the external problem causing your feelings.

4

How to Forgive and Forget

The final step in dealing with anger, and perhaps the most crucial one, is to forgive and forget. Matthew 6:15 warns, "But if you do not forgive others their trespasses—their reckless and willful sins, leaving them, letting them go and giving up resentment—neither will your Father forgive your trespasses" (AMP).

Often people have misconceptions about what forgiveness really is. Many of us, when trying to forgive someone, try to talk ourselves into thinking that what the other person did wasn't really wrong, or that he didn't really mean to do it, or that we overreacted to what he did. This may sometimes be the case, but at other times we need to fully recognize that what the other person did was definitely wrong, but that we will nevertheless forgive him and forget it, no matter how much he has hurt us.

Forgiving means that we actively choose to give up our grudge despite the severity of the injustice done to us. It does not mean that we